THINK HAPPY

THINK HAPPY

Instant Peptalks to Boost Positivity

KAREN SALMANSOHN

best-selling author of *Instant Happy*

TEN SPEED PRESS
Berkeley

Introduction

Words are powerful things. It's actually appropriate to call words "things"—even though you can't **see** words.

After all, words have weight. They can drag you down.

Words have height. They can lift you up.

Words have length. They can last a lifetime.

We have to be wildly watchful of the words we use—knowing that once these words go into our heads, it's super hard to get 'em out of there! I know that eventually the words I use most often to talk about my life will become either a supportive inner voice or an inner bully.

Ditto with the words we say to others. Our words have the power to lift people up—or put them down. Our words can inspire confidence—or obliterate it. So we must choose our words wisely. Over time, the words of all the various cheerleaders and critics we've had in our lives become our inner cheerleaders and inner critics. Basically, we gotta watch the words we think, speak, and listen to—because eventually these words create the world we see!

With this in mind, I'm excited for you to start using this book, so you can begin giving yourself the right words, at the right time. I call these motivating words "instant peptalks." I recommend using them on a daily basis—or an insomniacal 3 a.m. basis.

This collection of positive peptalks will quickly become your favorite go-to tool for whenever you need a little extra oomph and support.

The facts: A range of neuroscientific studies support how positive affirmations, when consistently repeated, can wind up sinking into the subconscious mind—thereby affecting a person's sense of self and their behavior.

The advantages of these 50 instant peptalks over regular ol' affirmations: These peptalks are far catchier and more logically convincing than mere affirmations—making them more liable to linger in your mind. Like a catchy song you can't stop humming, you will find yourself instinctively playing these peptalks in your head as helpful reminders to keep on moving forward.

The result: When used regularly, these peptalks will change your neural pathways, so you are more inclined to think optimistic thoughts, which lead to positive habits, which lead to a positively happier life!

My mission: This book will become your "inner power tool" for staying strong, confident, and happy—no matter how much you-gotta-be-friggin'-kidding-me life throws at you! A quick flip-through will help you find the right words to say during a challenging time, to yourself or to a loved one.

Throughout my life I've experienced how the right turn of phrase can be very powerful. When I was a child, my mom used to say: "If you do what you always do, you'll get what you always get." Such a simple phrase—yet it has continued to influence me throughout my life. Now as a mom myself, I use this exact peptalk with my son! In fact, all of the peptalks in this book are awesome to use with children. They'll permanently absorb these uplifting words—then wind up growing up with an inner cheerleader as their inner voice—instead of an inner fearleader.

As Muhammad Ali once said: "It's the repetition of affirmations that leads to belief. And once that belief becomes a deep conviction, things begin to happen."

Or as I like to say: "Sometimes you gotta fake positivity till you make positivity."

These mindfully crafted peptalks have served me well to stay strong and full of faith in all that life has to offer. I hope they'll also bring you impenetrable resilience to keep moving forward—and upward!

XO
Karen

5

THINGS TO SAY

WHEN *trying*

SOMETHING NEW

(and thereby scary)

PEOPLE WHO ARE HIGHLY AWESOME AT SOMETHING DIDN'T START OFF HIGHLY AWESOME. So don't compare your beginning to someone else's middle or advanced state.

It's okay to make mistakes, to fail, to struggle. What's not okay is to think that mistakes, failure, and struggle are permanent states of being! They're simply a bridge you must cross to get to the Land of the Highly Awesome.

Many highly awesome people have crossed this bridge:

- Twenty-two-Olympic-medal-winning swimmer Michael Phelps was at first afraid to put his face in the water.

- Bill Gates's very first business, Traf-O-Data, failed before he founded Microsoft.

- Walt Disney was fired once because he "lacked imagination and good ideas."

Remember: Your thoughts are either poison or nourishment. Choose them wisely. Make sure your optimistic, self-loving thoughts wildly outnumber your doubts and fears.

EVERY EXPERT STARTED OUT AS A BEGINNER

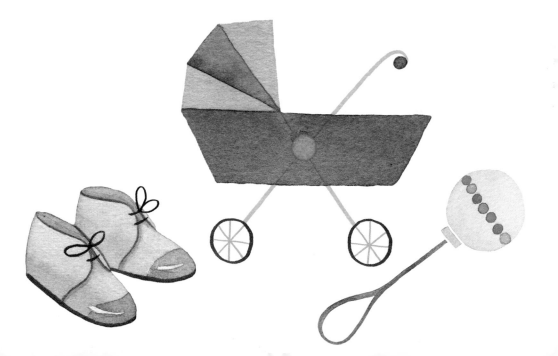

Practice is
how you learn

· ·

THIS IS A POWERFUL PHRASE TO SAY WHEN YOU'RE ATTEMPTING TO MASTER SOMETHING NEW. It's a reminder to stop being upset at every slipup—because you recognize it's part of the learning curve.

If you ever find yourself on a particularly roller-coaster learning curve, pause and repeat: "Practice is how you learn!"

Tip: Repeat this peptalk a few times *before* you start something new—as a warmly worded warm-up—to make sure your ego stays limber enough to handle whatever might come your way.

Author and researcher Geoffrey Colvin praised the power of practice in his book *Talent Is Overrated*. He shares a range of studies supporting how the true secret behind most inspiring success stories is *not* talent—but rather demanding, deliberate practice.

· ·

I LOVE COFFEE. IT'S MY BFF BEVERAGE. WHENEVER I NEED TO CONQUER PROCRASTINATION, I TURN TO CAFFEINATION.

One day I realized that fear offers the same energy surge as coffee. Both give an adrenaline rush, speed up breathing, and get neurons super-firing. In fact, fear—when channeled properly—could become my BFF too. It offers an espresso shot of fuel and awareness to do what I gotta do.

Fear is actually a helpful survival instinct—a tool from caveman days to help us act more boldly and run more quickly.

When I began thinking of fear as "nature's caffeine," I became braver. Now when I'm faced with a scary work project—or scary situation of any kind—I rename what I'm facing as *exciting*. Plus, instead of viewing myself as fearful, I think of myself as being in *extra energy mode*.

THREE

Fear is

NATURE'S CAFFEINE

FOUR

It's easier to be a
saint for fifteen
minutes than an hour

WANT TO CREATE HUGE CHANGE? Do a good habit for fifteen minutes daily. After all, it's much easier to be a saint for fifteen minutes than for many looooong hours.

Quickie examples: I do a fifteen-minute workout every morning on an indoor bike, and a fifteen-minute cleanup every night, wiping down and organizing our home.

The Japanese love this concept of little steps adding up to big improvement. They call it *kaizen.* Brain researchers Sandra Aamodt and Sam Wang are also kaizen fans. They believe if you train to do a task for fifteen minutes daily, eventually you'll be able to easily do it for far longer, because you're strengthening your brain's neural pathways—and thereby strengthening your "willpower muscles."

Meaning? For a tush of steel, exercise your tush muscles a little daily! For a discipline of steel, exercise your discipline muscles a little daily.

MANY PEOPLE LOVE DOING AFFIRMATIONS TO STAY POSITIVE. (EXAMPLE: "I AM MAKING LOTS OF MONEY.")

But sometimes one-size-fits-all affirmations aren't effective—particularly when you're highly curmudgeonly, which is when you most need a mood boost.

Fluffy affirmations can sometimes make you feel worse, because you become aware of how you're not living up to their hyperbolic hype.

The solution? Pour yourself a cockytale—a delicious blend of persuasive happy facts and/or marvelous memories—prepared just for you.

Quickie examples: You might pour yourself a cockytale about that time you slam-dunked a project or scored wildly well on a test.

Remember: High self-esteem is the opposite of fear and doubt. Hence, when you remind yourself of persuasive facts and convincing memories, you feel less anxious.

Warning: Don't let cockytales go to your head and get drunk on self-aggrandizement! Sip cockytales with the proper amount of food for thought.

POUR yourself A

"COCKYTALE"

5
THINGS
TO SAY
WHEN *feeling*
GRUMPY

GOOD NEWS: IF YOU CAN DRIVE YOURSELF CRAZY, YOU CAN DRIVE YOURSELF HAPPY. It's all about which thoughts you choose to think. Wherever thoughts go (toward crazy versus happy) is where you drive yourself.

When you realize how thoughts work like steering wheels, you're more likely to mindfully steer clear of negative thinking—knowing that will take you on a trip to nowhere. Or worse, crash you into unhappy circumstances.

Awesome metaphor: Racecar drivers know not to look at walls or obstacles. Why? Because wherever the driver looks is exactly where that racecar aims itself. Successful drivers diligently keep their eyes on where they want to go!

Your assignment: If you feel your thoughts swerving toward obstacles, doubts, or self-loathing, put on the brakes. Then refocus on what's going wonderfully right in your life—and where you want to be going.

ONE
. . .

THOUGHTS
are like
A STEERING
WHEEL

TWO

Being
NEGATIVE
is like SPRAYING
YOURSELF WITH
ANTI-CHARISMA

MANY QUANTUM PHYSICISTS BELIEVE NEGATIVE THOUGHTS AND WORDS HAVE NEGATIVE ENERGY VIBRATIONS, which can be felt in a larger universal energy field. Plus they believe these "negative vibes" can attract negative life circumstances.

Whether you believe in metaphysical "energy vibes" or not, it's only logical that being negative is like spraying yourself with anti-charisma!

Happily, the opposite is also true. Happy thoughts can create happy energy and happy vibes.

Basically, just as there's alluring sexual attraction (which people feel, but can't see), there's also negative energy repulsion (ditto).

When you think about the energy you emit this way, you're less likely to want to be negative, because you know how negativity dims your vibration. Instead, you'll be more motivated to think happy thoughts—and shine on.

• •

IF YOU WANT TO BE HAPPY, YOU MUST ACCEPT THAT EVERYTHING IN LIFE COMES WITH A POOPER SCOOPER FACTOR. EVEN GOOD, HAPPY STUFF.

Think about what happens when you get a cute puppy. You're immediately excited about all the fun and lovin' to come.

Then you have to train your puppy—and you realize, "Ahhh, yes, my adorable puppy comes with a yucky pooper scooper factor."

But because you love your puppy, you accept that some pooper scoopering is involved.

Similarly, your awesome life is full of infinite reasons to smile, yet it also comes with daily frustrations. Instead of sweating, resisting, and whining about the small stuff, just think of it as the pooper scooper factor of life.

• •

THREE

EVERYTHING
in life comes with
A POOPER
SCOOPER
FACTOR

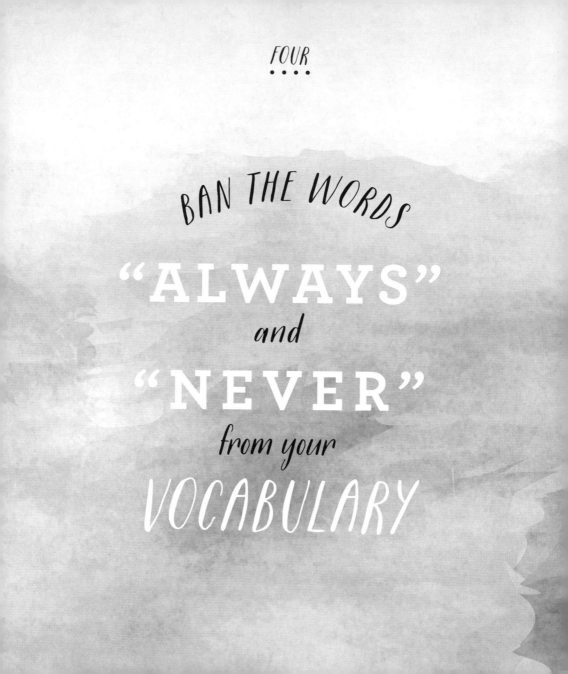

WHENEVER SOMEONE SAYS THEY'RE DEPRESSED, I TRY TO HELP THEM DRILL DOWN TO THE PESKY "ALWAYS" OR "NEVER" LURKING IN THEIR SUBCONSCIOUS OR CONSCIOUS MIND.

Quickie examples: "There are never opportunities for people my age." "Love never lasts for me—or anybody." "People always cheat in relationships."

Psychologists call these beliefs "permanent" and "pervasive"—and they're wildly dangerous. Any time you voice that "always" or "never," you're setting up a self-fulfilling prophecy of doom and a mindset of gloom.

The truth: Our "never" or "always" is *very rarely* actually true. It's usually a highly exaggerated negative belief.

Your assignment: Put your "always" and "never" beliefs on trial! Cross-examine them like a tough attorney—dispute and discredit them.

WANT TO KNOW ONE OF THE BIG DIFFERENCES BETWEEN HAPPY PEOPLE AND GRUMPY PEOPLE?

Grumpy people are "negative evidence collectors"—dutifully looking for AWFUL things, people, and events to put into a mental folder labeled "Proof Life Is Awful."

Happy people are "positive evidence collectors," constantly looking for AWESOME things, people, and events to put into a mental folder labeled "Proof Life Is Awesome."

Because happy people collect AWESOME, not AWFUL, stuff, they notice more AWESOME stuff—and fill up their mental folders with lots of happy evidence that life is indeed AWESOME!

In summary: It's amazing how powerful changing your belief system about the world can be. When you change the way you look at the world, you change what you notice and create for yourself.

FIVE
• • •

Be a

POSITIVE
EVIDENCE
COLLECTOR

5 THINGS TO SAY

WHEN *dealing* *with* MAJOR CHALLENGES

LIFE'S CHALLENGES ARE A LOT LIKE WASHING MACHINES. THEY TWIST US UP AND KNOCK US AROUND, BUT IN THE END WE COME OUT BRIGHTER AND BETTER.

Granted, when we're in the midst of troubled times, we simply feel like we're being wrung through the wringer.

I remember during one challenging time, I joked to a friend that I wanted to fire my "guardian angel" for sleeping on the job. Sure enough, as time passed, I realized it was actually *me* who needed the wake-up call.

Eventually I realized my emotional pain was a helper, trying to stop me from sleepwalking through life, and— CLUNK—to alert me to make needed, beneficial changes. Looking back, I can see this troubled time as a time of true cleansing.

When you're going through troubled waters, ride those waves and keep going.

ONE

Sometimes you're taken into troubled
waters not to drown but to be cleansed

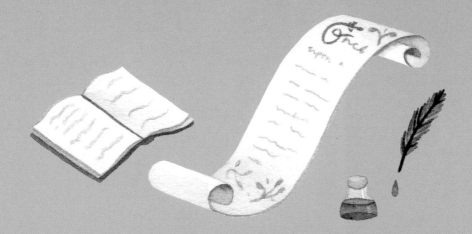

REJECTION. LOSS. ADVERSITY. WE FACE ALL KINDS OF CHALLENGES. You can't control what happens, but you can control the story you tell about it—and thereby change the effects on your future.

Your mission: Stop presenting your story as a sad one, and eventually it will stop being a sad story.

Your tools:

1. Give the story of your challenge (your breakup, job layoff, etc.) a positive title, like "The Gift" or "The Bridge" or "The Assignment."

2. When you wake up, get curious about what positive plot twists you're about to discover in your day that will bring you The Gift or The Bridge or The Assignment.

3. Turn crisis pain into crisis *fuel*. Get extra-motivated to turn your Plan B storyline into a happily ever after.

Remember: Often what feels like the end of the world is really a pathway to a far better place.

SOMETIMES OUR WORLD NEEDS TO BE UPENDED TO ALLOW US TO BETTER NOTICE ALL OUR INVISIBLE BLESSINGS—the people, things, and attributes we've become so accustomed to having that we've become blind to how blessed we are.

Basically, a big shake-up in our life can help to knock us out of our repeated cycles of thinking and behaving. We switch over to a new, groovier "brain groove" track—one that brings us better ways of seeing, being, and doing.

Plus, shake-ups can force us to let go of what we've been holding onto too tightly (negative relationships, toxic friends, unhealthy habits, unloving beliefs), freeing us to reach for something far better. Later we can see that "bad-luck" event was really a lucky turnaround.

WHEN YOUR WORLD GETS TURNED UPSIDE DOWN

VIEW IT FROM A NEW PERSPECTIVE

Be your own

SUPERHERO

IMPORTANT REMINDER DURING TOUGH TIMES: NOBODY'S COMING TO SAVE YOU. YOU HAVE TO SAVE YOURSELF. YOU HAVE TO BE YOUR OWN SUPERHERO.

(Although it's okay to be open to having a sidekick.)

You have to tap into that superpower deep inside you and know you are stronger than your challenges—and your challenges are making you stronger.

Know this now: Often life gives you challenges specifically based on what you most need practice in. *Especially* if you're facing a repeated pattern of pain. In fact, life will keep sending you the same problem over and over (and over) again—until you hero-up and choose to bravely face your inner demons and learn that darn lesson!

IF YOU COULD LIVE FOR TEN YEARS IN TOTAL BLISS—PAIN-FREE—BUT NOT REMEMBER ANY OF IT, WOULD YOU?

Aristotle says, say NO. He believed true happiness comes from gaining insight and growing into your best self. Otherwise you experience only immediate gratification, which is fleeting and doesn't grow you as a person.

The pain-free scenario mirrors someone doing crack or binge-drinking. It feels like you're avoiding pain and seeking bliss, but long-term you're *not* enjoying real life. You're numbing yourself, blocking yourself from life's inevitable ebbs and flows—which bring empowering insights that grow you into who you are.

So how do you morph an uncomfortable *is* into an inspiring isn't-so-bad? Tap into the power of silence—meditating, journaling, or going for long quiet walks. Silence is an awesome teacher. Get quiet and allow yourself to know what you need to know—to grow how you need to grow.

It is what it is—but YOU have the

POWER

to turn it into an isn't-so-bad

5
THINGS
TO SAY

WHEN FACED

with FAILURE

IF YOU WANT THE MINDSET OF A HAPPY, SUCCESSFUL PERSON, YOU MUST BE WHAT DR. CAROL DWEICK CALLS AN "INCREMENTAL THEORIST": someone who views talent as a stretchable skill set to be increased incrementally.

Unfortunately, many people are "entity theorists," attributing success to an innate, unalterable level of ability—a limited "entity" of talent. Entity theorists say things like: "I was born with that talent." "I'm a natural at this!"

So when entity theorists are faced with failure, they get discouraged, thinking it must be a lasting defect—a lack of ability that will forever block them from happiness and success.

Your assignment: When facing failure, remember Thomas Edison: "Results? Why, man, I have gotten lots of results! If I find 10,000 ways something won't work, I haven't failed. I am not discouraged, because every wrong attempt discarded is often a step forward."

CELEBRATE

EFFORT,

NOT

OUTCOME

There's a

GAIN

in EVERY

PAIN

EVERY TIME YOU LOSE SOMETHING, FAIL SOMETHING, BREAK SOMETHING, HURT SOMETHING, REPEAT:
"There's a gain in every pain." Next, get curious instead of furious. Search for the lesson in your pain.

Remember: It's okay to mess up—or feel messed up. You just can't lounge around in the mess. You gotta get up, dust yourself off, and seek out the message in the mess-up.

A mistake is a mistake only if you don't bother to seek out its lesson, meaning, and purpose.

WHEN I SAY "NEVER GIVE UP," I LOVE SAYING IT THREE TIMES, IN A FUNNY, WINSTON CHURCHILL—TYPE VOICE. (HUMOR IS AN ADDED STRESS RELIEVER.)

Psychologist Albert Bandura detailed fascinating research in *Self-Efficacy: Toward a Unifying Theory of Behavioral Change*: when you believe in your ability, you tend to not give up—which leads to success.

Example: Someone gives you a key from a huge pile and says, "This probably *won't* open this treasure chest." You try, but not very hard, because you don't expect it to work. And it doesn't. Next, they give you a single key: "*This* is the right one!" You believe. You try harder. The chest opens! Guess what? Both were the right key. But with the second, you had self-efficacy on your side—and you didn't give up.

Tip: Never give up—*unless* something's not working. Then breathe, think, create a new strategy, and try again.

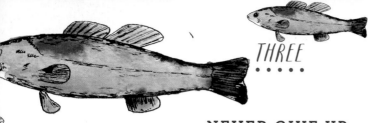

THREE

NEVER GIVE UP.

NEVER GIVE UP.

NEVER

GIVE

UP.

. . . .

"I BELIEVE IN YOU." "I BELIEVE IN MIRACLES." "I BELIEVE IN BETTER POSSIBILITIES."

There are many ways you can use the word "believe" to stay uplifted and aimed forward. Whatever phrase you choose, the concept of "believing" is a gift that keeps on giving.

Funny story: I say "I believe in you!" to my son, Ari, all the time. Recently I was ransacking our apartment for my cell phone. I collapsed on the sofa, frustrated. Suddenly I felt a tug on my yoga pants. It was Ari.

"Mommy, I know you can find your cellphone. *I believe in you.*"

His adorably serious words were just the shot of adrenaline I needed to stand up and try pulling the sofa away from the wall for a quick peek behind. Eureka! I found my lost cell phone!

Yep! I'm a big believer in the propulsion power of *believing.*

. . . .

FOUR
· · · ·

I
BELIEVE IN
_____

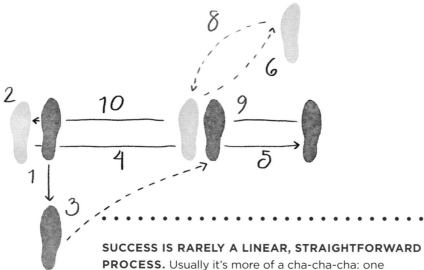

SUCCESS IS RARELY A LINEAR, STRAIGHTFORWARD PROCESS. Usually it's more of a cha-cha-cha: one step forward, two steps back; three steps forward, one step back.

Successful people are highly adaptable. When they stumble, they turn it into a dance move. When facing an obstacle, they find a way to dance around it.

In fact, every successful person in the world has two surprising things in common:

1. Failure.

2. Rejection.

Every member of the Fortune 500 Club could easily be a member of the Misfortune 500 Club. The big difference between these two groups? Fortune 500 members see failure as a helpful experience. They just keep on moving forward, knowing that at times this means taking a step backward. And most important of all, they know to never leave the dance floor.

Sometimes you have to

CHA-CHA-CHA

your way to getting

WHAT YOU WANT

5 THINGS TO SAY

TO IMPROVE *your*

"SELF-LOVE LIFE"

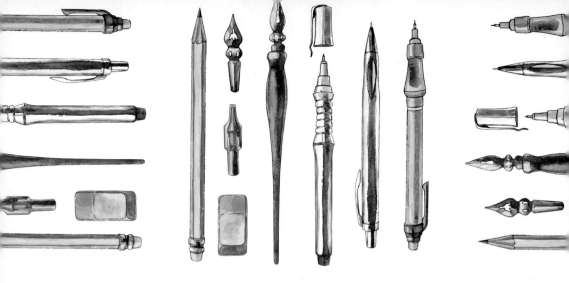

GOING FOR EXCELLENCE IS MOTIVATING. GOING FOR PERFECTION IS SETTING YOURSELF UP FOR PAIN—BECAUSE PERFECTION DOES NOT EXIST.

So be gentle with yourself. You're doing the best you can. You're simply a work in progress. And all those mistakes you make along the way have the power to turn you into something better, stronger, wiser than you might have been otherwise.

Remember: Your relationship with yourself sets the tone for every other relationship you have. So make it a warm and forgiving relationship. Talk to yourself the way you'd talk to someone you love. Shush your inner bully. Be your own bestie. Ban, delete, shred, obliterate the words "I'm not good enough."

Be good to you.

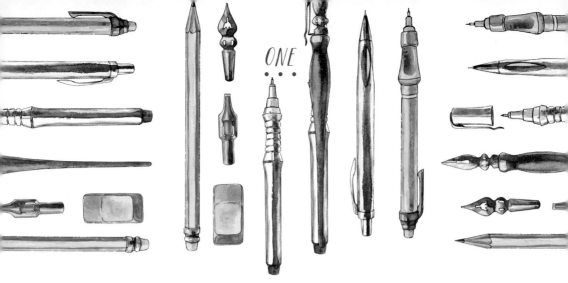

PERFECTIONISM
is a form of self-abuse

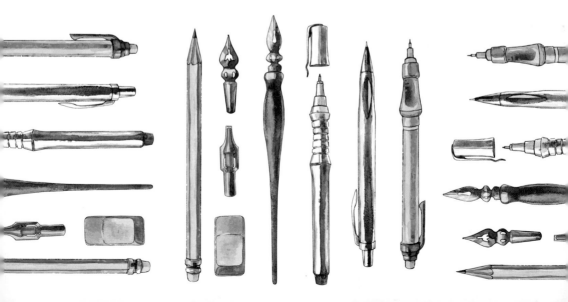

YOU ARE NOT A
PRETZEL

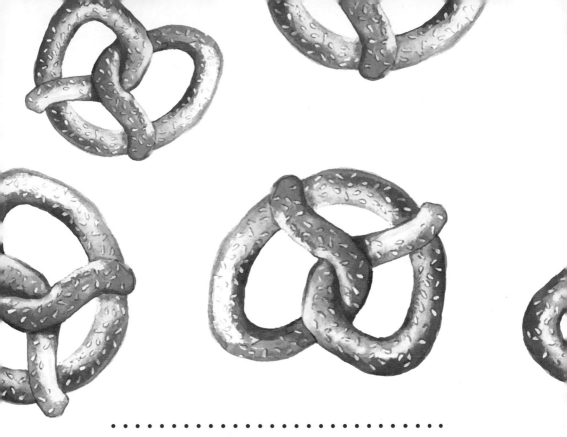

· ·

**YOU ARE NOT A PRETZEL. SO DON'T TWIST
YOURSELF INTO WHO YOU THINK PEOPLE WANT
YOU TO BE, JUST TO MAKE THEM HAPPY. THIS
MAKES YOUR SOUL FEEL ALL TWISTY-LIKE.**

Don't change yourself, ever—just to make someone
happy—unless that someone is you.

Be who you are. Accept and love all your quirks.

Don't be a pretzel. Be your whole enchilada.

· ·

YOU SHOULD ALWAYS RESERVE YOUR TIME FOR THE PEOPLE WHO MAKE YOU FEEL LIKE THEIR FAVORITE ITEM ON THE MENU.

And don't fret if someone doesn't like you. It's not other people's job to like you. It's yours.

Besides, there are even people out there who don't like cupcakes!

If you want to be happy, you don't need to surround yourself with lots of friends. You just need to find a few who love you lots.

Your mission: Surround yourself with people who make your soul feel happily caffeinated.

No matter how awesome you are, you won't be everyone's cup of tea—but no worries. You'll be many people's double espresso.

WEIRD
is the NEW
AWESOME

**BE PROUD OF WHATEVER MAKES YOU WEIRD—
BECAUSE THAT'S YOUR SOUL'S LIGHT SHINING
THROUGH.**

Remember: You get only one soul, and it's the only soul
of its kind on this vast planet—hence its weirdness. So be
good to your weird lil' soul.

Treat your soul like a soul mate. Take it for long walks.
Listen when it whispers its desires. Take action on what it
says is right—and right for you.

Never dim your soul's light for anyone—even if they make
you feel bad that it's shining too brightly in their eyes.
In fact, be sure to shine your special little soul's light as
brightly as possible—so other weirdos from your soul's
tribe can be sure to find you.

WHEN YOU DO GOOD, YOU FEEL GOOD—AND WHEN YOU FEEL GOOD, YOU DO GOOD. This is not only fun to say, it's researched information—with its own fancy name! It's called the "feel-good, do-good" phenomenon.

Studies show that when people feel good about themselves, they tend to do more good deeds, which then raises their self-esteem, which then makes them feel even happier, which then makes them want to do even more good— and on and on this cycle recycles itself!

So if you're feeling down, perform an act of kindness. Not only will your kindness make someone feel happier—you'll feel happier too.

Warning: This cycle works in reverse—as a "feel-bad, do-bad" phenomenon. If you're unhappy, you can become unhappier by indulging in bad behavior. Don't downward spiral! Instead, do a good deed and upward spiral to a happier mood.

Do good to feel good

5 THINGS TO SAY

WHEN *dealing* with *TOXIC PEOPLE*

SOME PEOPLE HATE YOU ONLY BECAUSE OTHER PEOPLE LOVE YOU. It's often a compliment when someone's trying to bring you down. They're trying to diminish what you have, because they think you have too much, and they wish they had more.

To illustrate with a tale someone once told me: A wise woman and her disciple were walking down a road. Suddenly an angry man in a carriage drove haphazardly by, pushing the woman into a ditch filled with muddy water.

The woman called after him, "May you have everything you want!"

The disciple, surprised, asked, "Why did you say that nice thing to a man with such horrible behavior?"

"Because a happy man wouldn't have thoughtlessly pushed someone into a ditch."

The lesson: If you want to be happy, silently send love to this person, hoping they find their way to inner peace. Then redirect your thoughts where the most peace is found.

If someone is trying to

PULL YOU DOWN,

it just means they are beneath you

NEVER LET
A ZOMBIE BITE
TURN YOU INTO
A ZOMBIE

· ·

IF SOMEONE'S HURT YOU DEEPLY, IT'S TEMPTING TO WANT TO SHUT DOWN—AND NOT JUST FOR A WEEK, OR A MONTH, BUT FOREVER.

It's like a zombie movie: A soulless zombie takes a chomp out of someone innocent. The bitten one becomes zombielike. Their soul shuts down. They crave darkness. They want to bite others.

Likewise, when you've suffered an emotional zombie bite, it's tempting to join the zombie crowd, seek dark thoughts, and start chomping others. It's especially tempting to chomp the zombie chump who chomped you!

Here's how to resist—and keep your soul alive:

1. Face toward the light of love, forgiveness, and growth.

2. Remember, your zombie was bitten by a zombie who was bitten by a zombie—and so on. *You* can save the planet from a zombie takeover by making sure you never become a zombie yourself!

· ·

· ·

IF SOMEONE TREATS YOU WITH DISRESPECT, GET THEM OUT OF YOUR LIFE.

If you experience a parade of disrespecting people, get this painful pattern out of your life!

How? Dig deep into your psyche. Explore why you feel most comfortable feeling uncomfortable.

Perhaps as a child you learned that love comes with pain or disrespect—so too much peace and support makes you anxious. Basically, the level of joy and love you grew up with becomes the level you seek. If this happiness concentration shifts—even upward—it feels unfamiliar. So you may instinctively self-sabotage to shift your happiness concentration back to your familiar zone. Or you may always choose people who bring familiar pain.

Helpful meditation: "I am not my past. I am not how others once treated me. I am only who I think I am right now in this moment."

· ·

You are a fine piece of china.
Don't let anyone treat you
like a paper plate.

Every
JERK HAS A
SILVER LINING

THERE ARE ALWAYS PERKS TO LEARN FROM JERKS. A BIGGIE: THEY REMIND YOU TO NOT BE ANYTHING LIKE THEM.

If someone hurts you, train your brain to refocus on being proud of NOT being someone who behaves so badly. Choose to be kind. Yes, even to jerks. Let them be a jerk. You be a kind person.

Although you can't always control what happens to you, you can control your response. You can choose the role of victim—focusing on blame, anger, regret, and resentment— or the role of victor—growing who you are, healing your wounds, retrieving your power, and moving forward stronger and wiser.

When you choose being a victor, you can become a teacher of your experience, not just a student. You can turn pain into purpose—and become of service to others.

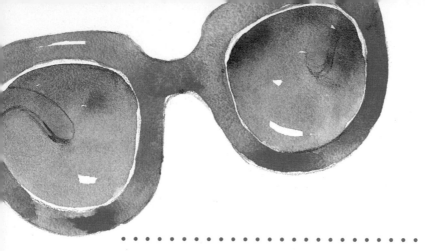

DON'T WASTE YOUR ENERGY ON HATE AND RESENTMENT; INVEST IT IN LOVE AND CONTENTMENT. Become so busy loving your life, there's no time for hate or bitterness.

A Japanese folktale: Once upon a time there was a happy little dog who loved to wag his tail. He came to a house, peeked inside, and saw a thousand other happy dogs, tails wagging hard.

He thought, "Wow! What a wonderful place. I must visit often!"

Another dog was less happy. He often growled at passersby. He too visited the house—and saw a thousand unfriendly dogs all growling at him!

He thought, "What a horrible place. I'll never go back!"

Why did each see a different house of dogs? Because it was a house of mirrors!

The lesson: Wherever you go, there you are. So wherever you go, go there with love.

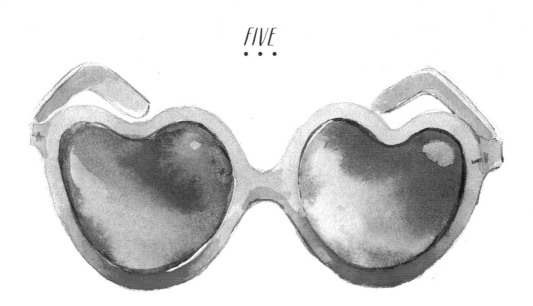

You can't see your
HATERS
when you've got your
love glasses on

5 THINGS TO SAY

WHEN *you feel* STRESSED OUT

I LOVE THIS METAPHOR ABOUT STRESS. A TEACHER WALKS AROUND THE CLASSROOM WITH A GLASS OF WATER.

The students expect the teacher to ask: "Is this glass *half empty or half full*?"

Instead, she asks, "How heavy is this glass of water?"

The students guess anywhere from eight to twenty ounces.

The teacher smiles, then explains, "The actual weight doesn't matter. It all depends on how long I hold it. If I hold it for a minute, it's not so heavy. If I hold it for a few days, my arm will feel paralyzed. Your stresses are like this glass of water. If you think about them a little, you won't be so affected. But if you think about them a lot, you'll feel great pain."

The lesson: If you want to lower your stress, lower your glass full of worry.

EACH DAY
*has only a certain
amount of time –*
DON'T WASTE
it STRESSING
*over things you
can't control*

Dorothy never said
there was no place like office

· ·

YO! IT'S CALLED AN OCCUPATION—NOT A PREOCCUPATION!

It's called success—not obsess.

It's called "the weekend"—not "be weakened from working nonstop."

It's called giving yourself a break to avoid a breakdown.

It's called being balanced, centered, and good to yourself.

· ·

• •

RECENTLY I HAD A COMPUTER MALFUNCTION. MY GO-TO TECH GENIUS TOLD ME to unplug my computer—then restart it. As soon as I refreshed my laptop, everything worked fine.

Afterward, I thought about how helpful this "unplug it" strategy is for all of life's problems. I often think my wisest, clearest, and most creative thoughts after a nice walk or a relaxing bubble bath.

There are some interesting neuroscientific reasons why unplugging recharges. When you're stressed, your brain enters into "fight or flight"—and gets stuck in its less smart "reptilian brain" setting. This is why people under great stress feel tongue-tied and choked up. The "smarter" neocortex and limbic aspects of their brain are being locked out. When you do something to de-stress, you exit "fight or flight" and tap back into your smarter-thinking neocortex and limbic system.

• •

THREE

"ALMOST EVERYTHING
WILL WORK BETTER IF
YOU UNPLUG FOR A FEW
MINUTES—INCLUDING YOU."
–ANNE LAMOTT

FOUR

Find the humor

ONE OF THE MOST SELF-LOVING ACTS YOU CAN DO IS FIND HUMOR IN A STRESSFUL SITUATION. It's tough to feel anxious or sad when you're belly-laughing. And simply smiling or being silently amused has proven mood-boosting benefits.

Psychologists Herbert Lefcourt and Rod Martin at the University of Waterloo found that stressed-out people with a strong sense of humor become less depressed and anxious than those whose sense of humor is less well developed.

Researchers Mary Payne Bennett and Cecile Lengacher at West Chester University in Pennsylvania found that students who used humor to cope were more likely to be in a positive mood.

That's just the tip of the whoopee cushion! Laughter also . . .

- Increases endorphins and dopamine

- Increases relaxation response

- Reduces pain and tension

- Increases resilience and optimism

Your assignment: Watch a funny movie. Go to a comedy club. Spend time with kids—or childish, silly adults.

SELF-CARE IS NOT SELFISH CARE. IF YOU PUT YOUR EMOTIONAL NEEDS ON A BACK BURNER, YOU'RE GOING TO FEEL BURNT OUT.

It's essential to maintain healthy boundaries. You need to put your lips together and say that tongue-twister: NO.

Self-care can be particularly tough for parents. It's easy to forget about our needs when we're taking care of our kids. It's funny how we'd never think of depriving our children of time to play, laugh, relax, and sleep. Well, parents need this too! All work and no play is soul-depleting.

Your assignment:

Stop being ruled by guilt.

Eat healthy meals, and get enough vitamin Zzzzzzs.

Make time to work out at the gym.

Make time to go inward in a spiritual practice.

Get enough me-time doing things you love.

Get enough we-time doing things with people you love.

You are not required

to **set yourself** *on*

FIRE *to* KEEP
OTHERS WARM

5
THINGS
TO SAY

WHEN *looking for*
and maintaining
LOVE

LOVE AT FIRST SIGHT IS EASY. IT'S LOVE AT 1,000,001ST SIGHT THAT'S TOUGH TO FIND.

Although love at first sight does happen, far too often it's only infatuation at first sight. It takes time to get to know someone's true inner self.

Your assignment: You know how health-conscious people read food labels to make sure there are no dangerous ingredients? If you want to find a healthy relationship, think of yourself as *emotionally* health conscious! Always take time to find out what's inside a yummy-looking, tempting person—before you let them into your emotional system.

Remember: Just because someone's packaged as mouthwatering, that doesn't mean they're good for you! Make sure they don't have "bad character ingredients"— which might create heart problems and headaches.

The good news: A person just gets yummier when you're attracted to their soul.

Don't look for a partner
who is eye candy.
Look for a partner who is
soul food.

JUST LIKE
you shouldn't go
food shopping
WHEN STARVING,
you should be careful
looking for love
WHEN LONELY

NEVER ALLOW LONELINESS TO DRIVE YOU INTO THE ARMS OF SOMEONE YOU DON'T BELONG WITH.
You gotta love your own company, so you choose people out of love for them, not fear of being alone.

Instead of being needy for love, you should be "want-y." You should *want* someone—because their presence enhances your already happy life. The less needy you are, the less likely you'll be to overlook red flags—or become unhealthily codependent.

PEOPLE TREAT YOU AS YOU EXPECT TO BE TREATED. IF YOU DON'T FULLY LOVE YOURSELF, YOU'LL SETTLE FOR PEOPLE WHO DON'T FULLY LOVE YOU.

You've probably heard of an "Achilles heel"—a weakness that leads to a downfall. Often love problems arise when you have an "Achilles something"—a feeling of weakness that makes you doubt your self-worth.

Examples: You feel insecure about your weight; you have an "Achilles tush." You feel insecure about your monetary stability—that's an "Achilles bank account." You feel insecure about your age—"Achilles wrinkles." If an Achilles something makes *you* feel less worthy, you need to learn to love yourself more—imperfections and all.

Assignment: Create what I jokingly call a "they should be so lucky to be with me" list. Write down all the good stuff you offer. Take your focus off your insecurities. Focus on the joy you bring!

Realize how much you're worth, and don't give people discounts

If it doesn't open, it's not your door

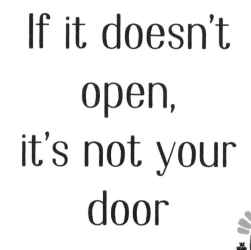

NOT EVERYONE YOU LOSE IS A LOSS. YOU DON'T NEED ANYONE WHO DOESN'T NEED YOU. So don't chase people who require being chased. If someone's a good catch, they'll want to be caught.

Even when you're at your best, you won't be good enough for the wrong person. In contrast, when you're at your worst, you'll still be worth it for the right person.

So if someone wants to leave, recognize that this doesn't mean it's a bad thing. It just means their part in your story is over. Your story will go on—with new love opportunities. Just focus on the lessons learned—and you'll be headed for a far happier relationship.

The good news: Every breakup is an opportunity to trade up. The empty space this person leaves behind is freed up for someone far more right!

WANT TO IMPROVE YOUR CHANCES OF FINDING A SOUL MATE? STOP SEEKING A "WISH LIST" OF QUALITIES (sexy, smart, funny, successful, etc). Instead, seek a "wish feeling." And the number one feeling you should be seeking—even before the feeling of love—is the feeling of safety.

If you don't feel safe with your partner (safe being your true self, safe expressing yourself, etc.), you will never feel true love. If you don't feel comfy being vulnerable, there can be no true intimacy.

Important reminder: In a healthy relationship, your partner won't want you to feel as if you're walking on eggshells. They'll want you to feel as if you're listening to seashells: calm, tranquil, secure!

In summary: It's called a soul mate—not an ego mate, wallet mate, lust mate, or status mate. Find a partner who makes your soul feel safe and happy.

FIVE

It's better to hold out
for a soul mate than settle
for a cell mate

5
THINGS
TO SAY
WHEN YOU NEED
TO FORGIVE
AND FORGET

CONFESSION TIME: I WAS A STRESS EATER UNTIL I LEARNED THAT WE CHOOSE TO OVEREAT (OR OVERSHOP OR OVERDRINK) to punish ourselves—for anger we're feeling at ourselves or someone else.

Basically, we seek addictions to avoid being fully present with uncomfortable feelings—or to punish ourselves because we're upset about how a negative situation unfolded.

Meaning? When I pigged out on a big bag of Cheese Doodles, I was really pigging out on a big bag of "I hate me for allowing that to happen Doodles" or "I hate that this toxic person/challenge/rejection happened to me Doodles."

Researchers at the University of Wisconsin comparing forgiveness therapy with traditional addiction therapy found that the forgiveness therapy helped relieve the urge for substance abuse even more successfully than the traditional.

Tip: Whatever your problem, the answer is never in the refrigerator.

ONE
· · ·

Don't hurt yourself

BECAUSE

YOU'RE ANGRY AT
SOMEONE ELSE

TWO

Hating someone makes
them important.
Forgiving them makes
them obsolete.

IF YOU REALLY WANT TO GET BACK AT SOMEONE WHO'S HARMED YOU, BECOME INDIFFERENT TO THEM. YOU'LL BE MAKING THEM OBSOLETE—THE BEST REVENGE OF ALL.

Important reminder: Forgiveness does not mean you approve of your offender's wrongdoing. Forgiveness is not viewing what someone did as less harmful than it was. Nor is it about giving your offender a free pass to continue that behavior.

Forgiveness is simply about recognizing that staying resentful creates an "active echo" of the pain your offender caused. By saying that your offender's awful offense is "beyond forgiving," you keep the offense alive in your heart.

Forgiveness begins with the mind recognizing that the past cannot be changed, but happily the present and future can be. Eventually forgiveness progresses to the heart, which decides it will no longer allow the offender's pain to take permanent residence there.

FORGIVENESS IS MAKING THE CHOICE TO RELEASE YOUR OFFENDER FROM A SPIRITUAL DEBT you feel they owe you, so you can invest your thoughts and energies more wisely—and not go into spiritual debt yourself because of mounting anger and resentment.

Your assignment: Cancel all perceived "spiritual debts." Write a list of offenses you feel your offender has committed. Cross out each one. Write "CANCELED" or "PAID IN FULL." Your life will feel richer because you'll have more time and energy to invest in love, laughter, and peace of mind.

Forgiveness is releasing someone
from a spiritual debt—
a debt you're the one stuck
paying for

When someone treats you badly,
it's because they feel bad

WHEN SOMEONE FEELS BAD INSIDE, THEY OFTEN WANT TO DO THINGS TO MAKE OTHERS FEEL BAD. In contrast, when someone feels happy on the inside, they want to do things to make others feel happy. This is why it's so important to make sure you feel good on the inside!

If right now you're upset because someone has been mean to you, it's helpful to remind yourself that it's because they feel bad inside. Take some time to better understand them—their childhood, their trauma, their mood. Don't do this to simply find excuses for them. Do it to help yourself heal—to depersonalize the pain. When you seek compassion for them, you wind up having more compassion for yourself, too.

In summary: When someone behaves badly, do not inhale their bad feelings. Breathe it all out—then let them inhale your inner peace.

WHEN YOU'RE EMOTIONALLY SUCKER-PUNCHED, IT'S NORMAL TO TAKE TIME ALONE TO HEAL AND GAIN INSIGHT. BUT MAKE SURE YOU'RE GOING INTO A HEALTHFUL "COCOON"—NOT A "CAVE."

A COCOON is a quiet, comfortable place where you evolve and regain energy to reemerge in your full power.

A CAVE is a quiet place you go to brood and growl, to hide from a cold, unsafe world.

How to tell the difference:

If your heart is light, you're in a cocoon, uplifting yourself with "butterfly stories" and doing "butterfly math" (1 untrustworthy person = 1 untrustworthy person).

If your heart is heavy, you're in a cave, depressing yourself with "bear stories" and doing "bear math" (1 untrustworthy person = a world of untrustworthy people).

Reminder: Never let someone's reckless behavior make you a recluse. Become a force to be reckoned with instead!

Don't mistake a cave for a cocoon

5

THINGS TO SAY

TO MOTIVATE YOURSELF TO

GO for YOUR

DREAMS

THE PURPOSE OF YOUR LIFE IS TO FIND AND PURSUE YOUR LIFE'S PURPOSE—YOUR SOUL'S PASSIONS. For some it's creating new technology, designing products, practicing medicine—and at least one person was put on this planet to invent that little plastic doohickey that holds up the pizza box lid.

Whatever your mission, make sure it's uniquely yours.

If someone tells you you can't accomplish your mission, recognize this is the tiny voice of their limited thinking. You must drown out their negative voices (and limiting choices) by raising the volume of your soul's voice.

You must be what I call "soul-istical"—which is very different from "egotistical." Soul-istical is when you're confident in your soul's power to achieve what you're here on this planet to do.

It's your path. Walk it. Run it. And keep on running—until that nay-saying becomes distant mutterings.

If people doubt how far you can go, go so far that you can't hear them anymore

Think of life as a competition with yourself to become extraordinary

I HAVE A PLATONIC CRUSH ON ARISTOTLE, THE GREEK PHILOSOPHER. I love his philosophy of why we're here on this planet: to grow into our best selves—to realize our fullest potential.

Aristotle believed each of us has a soul with unique gifts and passions. If we want to become our best selves, we need courage and discipline to keep getting better at our unique gifts and passions.

In other words, you are not here to learn how to become better than me or anybody else. You are here only to learn how to become better than who you were yesterday.

Because your thing is not my thing, there's enough room in this world for us all to do our thing.

Designer and blogger Ericka Cook said it well: "I'm not interested in competing with anyone. I hope we all make it."

· ·

MEDITATION ENERGIZES YOU AND HELPS YOU THINK MORE CLEARLY AND BE MORE PRODUCTIVE. SO DOES HAVING FUN. FUN IS MEDITATION ON STEROIDS.

Say I hand you a pint of ice cream and a spoon and say, "Finish this in one hour! I'll be back! It better be done!" I'm betting you'll get it done. Not because you had to force yourself to stay disciplined, but because you were having a good time.

Fun is a high-performance fuel for *everything* you need to do.

Plus, fun can make you smarter. Researchers at the University of Western Ontario studied the effects of watching funny videos versus sad news stories. Guess what? Watching fun stuff made people better at mental challenges like number puzzles.

Gallup studies show when you have a best friend at work, you're seven times more likely to be engaged in your job.

In summary: Don't work longer hours—work more *fun* hours.

· ·

THREE

Fun is a high-performance fuel

FOUR
. . . .

Don't shrink your dreams.

SUPER-SIZE
WHO YOU ARE.

REMEMBER HOW FRANK SINATRA SANG "DO BE DO BE DO"? FRANK WAS A GREAT CROONER, BUT A DYSLEXIC SELF-HELP GURU. To live your happiest life, you gotta sing "Be do be do be." You must focus first on *being*, then *doing*. Because who you *are* affects what you *do*—and how you do it.

For example, you may be thinking "I want to start a company." To achieve this goal, you must be disciplined, patient, organized, courageous, etc.

With this in mind, before you write a daily to-do list, write a *to-be* list. Jot down qualities you want to develop.

Next, as you do your to-do list, become aware of *being* these things.

It's good to regularly ask yourself: "Who do I need to become to get all that I want in life?"

In summary: To grow your success, grow who you are.

· ·

I'M A BIG FAN OF POSITIVE THINKING. But all the positive affirmations in the world won't work if you don't back up your positive thoughts with positive effort and consistent action.

If you want to get a lot, be ready to sweat a lot. The best things in life are on the exit ramp of your comfort zone.

1. Get clear on what you passionately want and need to do to get it. Schedule a six-month plan in your calendar. Remember, wishy-washy vague dreams bring about wishy-washy vague plans, which bring about wishy-washy lousy results.

2. Eleanor Roosevelt advises: Do something each day that scares you. Remember, there's no such thing as ready. Just start doing what you gotta do, and you'll become ready. Don't put it off till later—because later often becomes never.

· ·

FIVE

The law of *attraction*
doesn't work without the
law of *perspiration*

Image on page ii © Rudchenko Liliia/Shutterstock.com
Image on page iv © solarbird/Shutterstock.com
Image on pages 4—5 © AnnaC/Shutterstock.com
Image on page 8 © Maryna S/Shutterstock.com
Image on page 9 © Anastasiya Samolovova/Shutterstock.com
Image on page 10 © J.D.S/Shutterstock.com
Image on page 11 © Irina Oksenoyd/Shutterstock.com
Image on page 12 © Kanate/Shutterstock.com
Wings image on page 12 © xenia_ok/Shutterstock.com
Image on page 13 © 501room/Shutterstock.com
Life preserver image on page 16 © Eisfrei/Shutterstock.com
Wheel image on page 19 © Eisfrei/Shutterstock.com
Raindrops image on pages 18—19 © Magnia/Shutterstock.com
Perfume image on page 20 © Rudchenko Liliia/Shutterstock.com
Bubble images on pages 20—21 © Magnia/Shutterstock.com
Image on page 22 © Alexander Tihonov/Shutterstock.com
Image on pages 24—25 © TairA/Shutterstock.com
Image on page 31 © Katflare/Shutterstock.com
Image on pages 34—35, 39 © Regina Jershova/Shutterstock.com
Image on page 38 © colors/Shutterstock.com
Image on pages 44—45 © Tetyana Snezhyk/Shutterstock.com
Image on pages 46—47 © Katerina Izotova/Shutterstock.com
Image on pages 48—49 © Guz Anna/Shutterstock.com
Image on pages 54—55 © AlexGreenArt/Shutterstock.com
Image on pages 56—57 © Anastasia Nio/Shutterstock.com
Image on pages 58—59 © Irina Vaneeva/Shutterstock.com

Image on page 62 © Skorik Ekaterina/Shutterstock.com
Image on page 62 © WasntMary/Shutterstock.com
Image on pages 66—67 ©Michael Vigliotti/Shutterstock.com
Image on pages 74—75 © Moljavka/Shutterstock.com
Image on page 80 © Maria Zvonkova/Shutterstock.com
Image on page 81 © donatas1205/Shutterstock.com
Image on page 82 © TairA/Shutterstock.com
Image on page 83 © foxie/Shutterstock.com
Image on page 84 © Veronika M/Shutterstock
Image on page 85 © AnnaC/Shutterstock.com
Image on page 90—91 © Ka_Li/Shutterstock.com
Image on pages 96—97 © Nenilkime/Shutterstock.com
Image on page 98 © Undrey/Shutterstock.com
Image on page 99 © karavai/Shutterstock.com
Image on pages 102—3 © Nadydy/Shutterstock.com
Image on page 104 © KA-KA/Shutterstock.com
Image on page 105 © goldnetz/Shutterstock.com
Image on page 106 © TonTonic/Shutterstock.com
Image on page 107 © Angie Makes/Shutterstock.com
Image on page 108—9 © TairA/Shutterstock.com
Image on pages 112—13 © Eisfrei/Shutterstock.com
Image on pages 118—19 © Katerina Izotova/Shutterstock.com
Image on pages 120—21 © Eisfrei/Shutterstock.com
Image on page 122 © Oksana Boguslavska/Shutterstock.com
Image on page 123 © Jane_Lane/Shutterstock.com
Image on page 124 © Oksana Boguslavska/Shutterstock.com

Library of Congress Cataloging-in-Publication
Data is on file with the publisher.

Hardcover ISBN: 978-1-60774-962-2
eBook ISBN: 978-1-60774-963-9

Printed in China

Design by Margaux Keres and Nami Kurita
Cover illustration by Monica Garwood

10 9 8 7 6 5 4 3 2 1

First Edition